BORDERERS

Borderers

Diana Hendry

PETERLOO POETS

First published in 2001
by Peterloo Poets
The Old Chapel, Sand Lane, Calstock, Cornwall PL18 9QX,
U.K.

© 2001 by Diana Hendry

The moral rights of the author are asserted in accordance
with the Copyright, Designs and Patent Act, 1988

All rights reserved. No part of this publication may be
reproduced, stored in a retrieval system, or transmitted,
in any form or by any means, electronic, mechanical,
photocopying, recording or otherwise without the prior
permission in writing of the publisher.

A catalogue record for this book is available
from the British Library

ISBN 1-871471-90-7

Printed in Great Britain By
Antony Rowe Ltd, Chippenham, Wilts.

ACKNOWLEDGEMENTS

Acknowledgements are due to the editors of the following journals: *Ambit, Envoi, Markings, Mslexia, North, Phras '97, Poetry Review, The Scottish Book Trust, The Spectator, Thumbscrew.*

'Arkadi Monastery' won first prize in the 1996 Housman Society Competition. 'Seals', ' The Lost Memories of Llamas' and 'The Real and Unreal Scot' were highly commended in the Exeter Poetry Prize 1997 and 1998.

My grateful thanks to The Scottish Arts Council and to Dumfries & Galloway Royal Infirmary for a one-year residency. A particular thank-you to David Foreman, Dr. Lindsay Martin, Sister Liz Rae and the staff of the IT department.

At home – my thanks to Ursula, Rosie and Eddie for poems, suppers and support.

for Kate – with love

Contents

Page

HOSPITAL MATTERS

- 10   Hospital Scribe
- 11   Poem for a Hospital Wall
- 12   A Poem for Henry Who Doesn't Like Poems
- 13   Susanne
- 15   The Borderers
- 16   Last Days
- 19   Demon Lover
- 20   Tinsel Dreams
- 21   Tell-Tale
- 22   Poet's Prescription

ACROSS THE BORDER

- 24   Courting the River
- 26   The Real and Unreal Scot
- 27   The Stainless Scot
- 28   Without Trees on the Shetlands
- 29   Winter Journey
- 30   Seagulls

CREATURES

- 32   Seals
- 33   The Lost Memories of Llamas
- 35   Dog Days

AUNT ROMA & CO

- 38   Aunt Roma
- 39   The Children's Tale
- 40   The Fishwoman
- 41   Potato Cuts
- 42   The Long Count
- 43   To Kate at Twenty Five
- 44   After
- 45   Waiting

46 My Father's Chandelier
47 International Trader
48 Grandad
49 Grandma as a Genie
50 Wives
51 Quite
52 At Your Gate
53 Belonging

INNOCENCE & EXPERIENCE

56 Milk
57 Drinking Brandy on Whitstable Beach

HOMES & GARDENS

60 Estimates
62 The Painters
63 Angus
64 Lowry's House
65 Bulbs
66 Apple Sense
67 Eve Makis the Abject Serpent Serviable
68 Monterery Pine
70 Weeding Mrs. Baker's Garden

A FEW STRANGE CREATURES

74 The Cullen Skink
75 At Last I Decide to Speak to Fear Directly
77 The Enemy
78 Viva Health Club Blues

MYSTERIES

80 Reconstructing Heaven
81 Guide Book Angels
82 Without You
83 Arkadi Monastery
86 Jubilee Line

HOSPITAL MATTERS

Hospital Scribe

'Write it all down,' he says,
'from the beginning. The facts.'

We go through his Gorbals childhood,
his stint in the navy. The perks he had
from the catering trade. The money he made
from property sales. The final triumph
of the big country house. Seventy years
in ten-and-a-half pages. The heart's story's

hid like a walnut within. It's the day
he said, 'Mother, hold up your apron!'
and tipped in his first wages.
It's the kiss he stole from a girl in a lift.
That summer's five day bike-ride
to Cornwall with Jimmy. Tears
for his wife. Love for his sister.

I've got it all tidy, the caught life,
in chronological order when – 'I haven't
told you,' he says, 'about the time I smuggled
gold...' Then he's gone, story half told,
my pen in mid sentence, mystery
saving us both from ourselves.

Poem for a Hospital Wall

Love has been loitering
down this corridor.
Has been seen
chatting up out-patients,
spinning the wheels of wheelchairs,
fluttering the pulse of the night nurse,
appearing, disguised, as a bunch of grapes and a smile,
hiding in dreams,
handing out wings in orthopaedics,
adding a wee drappie
aphrodisiaccy
to every prescription.
No heart is ever by-passed by love.

Love has been loitering
down this corridor.
Is highly infectious.
Mind how you go. If you smile
you might catch it.

A Poem for Henry Who Doesn't Like Poems

(i.m. Henry Clement Smith)

Here's an invisible bunch of flowers.
They don't need a jug. Or water.
Keep them in your mind's eye
and they'll last forever. Look,

here's Lancashire daffs, not lightly
blown over and sturdy tulips, Yorkshire
bred. The bougainvillaea from Rhodes
could warm the winter. But best of all

the roses that you've grown.
They have your touch, your finger-print
in their petals. I've put in poppies,
multi-coloured, frail, but with the knack

of thriving in unlikely places –
like a poem, in fact.

Susanne

for Billy, Beu and Beth

I put your name in my address book
as if doing so would keep you here
among the living, practising
that kind of magic spell to do
with names – something of that same
desire that made us scrawl
'Kilroy was here' on city walls.

It's the manner of your being here
that's harder to explain. You were
a double Scotch, a concentrate
of zest and love. Perhaps that,
as much as cancer, wore you out.
Too live a wire. I don't want
to face the fact of tragic waste
or your two weans left behind.

And I won't do what death has done
and cross you out. Your name
can stay, though your address
has changed. I'd like to send
you this, if I knew where.
My guess is you'd reply
in fiercely spitting lines
about how that 'bastard cancer'
got you in the end and slit
the thin spun life. No doubt
you'd add instructions on how
best to love the children – when
to buy new socks, the importance

of cuddles. Susanne, I hope
It's all right now. I hope
your hair's grown back,
and your grin.

It's rained all summer here
because of you.

The Borderers

They take their time. Linger, on the border,
like women who go weeks beyond full term
or those who climb to the top of the cliff
then hesitate. What keeps them?
What holds them back? A tough
and worldly umbilical cord perhaps or
maybe the delay's at the other end
and they're caught in an out-patients queue
their names not called.

Relations wait, wipe spittle,
read the paper, pat a pillow,
hold an aloof hand, take tea

and grief, while they, the borderers,
cling on. Is what looks like dreaming
a final drama? Are they back
in childhood's summer? Do they struggle
with demons? Are they being shriven
by an advance party of angels?

It's like that moment when,
seeing off friends at the airport,
you're allowed no further. We wait

for the end, for the gentle finishing touch.
I'd like to think it's a rush of love to the brain,
then out. But when it's over, dream done,
breath drawn, it's us who're left in the dark.

Last Days

1.
Morphine's doused him
like sand a fire,
Henry Clement Smith
who was obstreperous,
who was not impressed
by the new-fangled
hospital bed
ironically called 'Pegasus';
who despite two kinds of cancer
kept his armour of selfhood on
but for a chink through which
his undoused spirit shone.

2.
What Molly implies
at eighty-five
is not just a youth mis-spent
but a whole life.
'How could anyone with good looks
and money, waste a whole life
on having a good time?' she asks,

happily.

3.
Eileen's stomach is as swollen
as if she was pregnant. She
calls it her water baby, nods off
over it. There's a daughter
not far away in miles
but terribly distant.
Eileen is finding her feet
in this new country

where climbing the stairs
is like mountaineering.

4.
He's not going to lie in bed.
Not him. He's up and dressed
and in the day room
with tea and fags,
his old shepherd's face
keen as a collie's.

'I'm Mr. Armitage,' he says,
letting you know
he's not to be trifled with.
His daughter's bought him
new slippers. Now he has
three pairs and a zimmer
who was the shepherd of the hill
seeing four hundred lambs
born in a season.

Alone and ill
he's on a different kind of hill
watching the corbies
gather on the dyke.

5.
God is getting in the way
of Angela's dying.
She's got enough to do
getting in and out of bed,
dealing with a bag of urine
strapped to her leg without
worrying about His purpose
or that biblical text –
'I shall do thee no harm'.

But what is His idea
of harm? They've cut out
her womb. The surgeon says
the bits of cancer left
are like grains of sand.

No-one mentions seeing infinity.

6.
Mavis thinks about her crystal
and what's to become of it.
The vase Jack bought
on their anniversary, the wee jug
she saw on holiday in Rhyl
and couldn't resist; the glass
basket, gift from a grandson.
All of it washed four times
a year and never used. But there.
In the corner. Catching light.

7.
Of Louise the Sister says,
'She's embarrassingly brave.'

Demon Lover

Not until someone tells you
he fancies you, do you see
that he's deadly attractive
and wildly promiscuous.
Very soon you're obsessed,
your life not your own,
always wondering when,
he'll seed, spread, touch bone.
You have therapy for infatuation,
the treatment makes you worse.
You try cutting him out of your life
but the cutting hurts. Poison
doesn't work. On some nights
you're wholly in his thrall.
He leaves you, of course –
and for days, weeks, months,
you begin to feel normal.

Then he's back, with that smile,
that dancer's way of metastazing
about your body – almost tenderly.
'I want you, I want you,' he moans,
and you can't resist. Somehow
you made him. Now you're his.

Tinsel Dreams

The room where they give you ECT
is at the far end. Afterwards
they give you tea on a verandah
like the ones in novels about TB.
You'll never know what you can't remember.

The staff encourage us to read
I'm OK You're OK though it's obvious
to anyone with half a mind – us,
that they are and we're not.
We spend whole afternoons making pots,

coil upon coil upon coil until
in-you-go – PLOP. At Christmas time
they banish all gloom and as ECT
has failed to cheer,
use tinsel to finish you off.

Tell-Tale

We met at the door.
She, the Sister from –
(let's be discreet, Ward ninety-four)
going one way and I the other.

She was blowing a pink bubble
of bubble gum.
It popped prettily as she said
'O don't make a poem out of this!'

As if I would.

Poet's Prescription

Rub sunshine into sore limbs.
Use Mozart ear-drops regularly.
Taste a poem a day.
Always keep a breath of Spring handy.

Wash eyes in wonder.

ACROSS THE BORDER

Courting the River

First thing, being a stranger
in a new town
is to introduce yourself
to the river. The locals,
the nearest post-office, pub,
place to buy paper – that
can all wait. But if you've
thoughts of staying around,
settling, being accepted,
it's essential you pay
your respects to the river
as you would if you landed
in the territory of some
great chief, or, more
particularly, his mistress.

Therefore go devoutly
over her bridges –
all of them, daily.
Speak to the seagulls.
Nod to the ducks. Imitate
that bow of the head
and neck the swans
have perfected. Walk,
in all weathers, along
her banks. Pay attention
to her moods; her highs
and lows – that tune
she plays, like wind
shuffling a forest. Do not
attempt a photo. It's true
that in abandoned moments

she'll let herself go
over the edge of the weir
in a slither of silk
but that's because flow
is what she's about and your
stills won't catch her.
Be sure to be there
when she puts on her moon-glossy
nightdress but be at home,
in bed, when out of bounds,
she's out on the town.

Be constant – as she's not –
in your attentions. Don't be
seduced into following her
to source or sea. Here's
where you're meant to be,
singing her praises. Watching.

The Real and Unreal Scot

The invisible man
who parks his car
outside my house every night
is a Real Scot.
It says so on his windscreen
and I believe it.
Often I lie in bed at night
imagining what a Real Scot
looks like.

His eyebrows are heavy
with generations.
His jaw is cleft
from the Stone of Scone.
Porridge and oatcakes
is his complexion.
His balls are the size
of Safeway haggis.
His hair is heather.
His kilt is tartan Swagger.
His bagpipes Wind and Lament.
His legs could leap the Cuillins,
take Princes Street in a single stride.

So huge is he
he'd have to fold himself in five
to squeeze inside
his grubby wee Metro.

Meanwhile
I've grown a tender spot
for the wry and subtle
unreal Scot.

The Stainless Scot

(for Tom Pow)

I reckon it was revenge.
I'm just five months over the border
– with my sapsy Southern vowels
and my unrolled Rs –
throwing a party
and it's neither Burns Night
nor Hogmanay
but he comes in a kilt
and is the only one to drink
red wine so that we're barely
into the champit tatties
when I'm down on my knees with a dish-cloth –
which is where all we English ought to be –
trying to wipe the blood
of red Rioja off his Campbell
and other anatomical parts
and I can hear the clang
of Highland warrior steel
hacking down my door and the ghost
of my Scottish ex laughing his Tam o' Shanter off
and saying whatever is the Gaelic equivalent of
'Gotcha!'

But in the morning, the kilted one
delivers a thank you note,
announcing himself as unblemished, 'stainless'.
Lord help me, but that was the trouble all along –

He was. I wasn't.

Without Trees on the Shetlands

Only an artist
uncertain of his lines
would add trees to this landscape –
such finery and frippery,
distracting the eye
from the true shape of things.

Here, where they've been rubbed out,
everything's clear.
A clean sweep, no frills,
no nonsense. No trees

and no doubt at all
your Maker
can get a better look at you.

Winter Journey

All the way to Scotland on the train,
haunted by the slow, hard dying of a friend,
I looked at newly-fallen snow and saw
only shrouds, the sheet pulled over the eyes,
anonymity, the sky's lid brought down.
So tried to see the kinder side of snow –

how it unites fields, eiderdowns
bare hills, reveals an underlying shape,
makes a plain post Ionic, ties
woolly love-knots in the barbed wire's twists;
how set against its clean white sweep,
a single sturdy figure's Indian inked.

O by the time the train arrived
I'd all my home-made comforts on:
Thermals. Snow boots. Blinkers. Hope.

Seagulls

I never thought to see the undersides
of a seagull's feet from underneath.
But up here, on the third floor
of *James Thin's* bookshop, Dumfries,
(poetry and children's) there's a daylong
seagull screech. It's like a protest
against whatever's lyric, sweet. The one
whose starfish feet I'm looking up at, squats
on a skylight. This town's more seagulls
than it wants. No-one loves them any more,
thinks them romantic, remembers Chekhov.
They've grown fat and greedy (haven't we all?)
their reputation sunk to 'rats with wings'.

I'm staying loyal to seagulls.
The untuned wildness of their call,
their seeming panic as if they've heard
some awful news, lost all their children,
can't find home. Theirs the last elegiac wail
of *The Seafarer* clenched in frosty angst
o'er his oars. Here, they monitor the river.
Perch on the edge of the century's weir. Take
from the top of a telegraph pole, a globally snooty
view of things; are a burst of snow feathers
from the sky's white pillow. I grew up with seagulls,
still believe they've something to tell us.

To scare the seagulls out of town
Talon Services are offering to fly
(in controlled conditions for three hours a day)
a falcon hawk. There's a plan
to prick eggs. I plot to open the skylight
to a skyful of seagulls. They could nest
with the poets and children. We might get the message.

CREATURES

Seals

Someone has stitched them up
in sleeping bags of stained grey satin.

They have a knowledge of legs
as we have of wings.

The clay of them's still soft. Slumbering
on the rocks, trying to harden into rock,

they're haunted either by a time
before they were fastened inside themselves

or by a time to come when their satiny pods
will pop and split and out they'll step

themselves, at last.

The Lost Memories of Llamas

They are making a bridge of rope
across a river in Machu Picchu.
Whether they are doing so
because there is a need for a bridge
or because an American anthropologist
wants to see how the Incas did it,
or for a television programme, isn't clear.
But at any rate, they are getting paid for it
and they come from their villages
in their lovely Peruvian hats,
arms braceleted in loops and coils
of stringy plaited reeds which are bound
into ropes, which are slung over the river,
which a team of men, laughing and joking,
haul, tug taught, and finally anchor.
It takes three days. The chief rigger,
(once a tightrope walker of distinction)
says it's a work of art and when the camera
draws back to show us the swoop of it –
this cat's cradle hung between mountains,
muscular, whiskery and wondrously patterned –
we see that it is. And that the beauty of the bridge
is not in its strength and steadiness but – as in all
attempts at connection – in its risk and sway.

The American anthropologist teeters nervously
across it. (She is wearing a not-so-lovely hat
and smiling a smile of terror.) 'I daren't
look down!' she cries. We want her to look down.
We want her to believe. In art. In the Incas.

In the connections. The llamas have lost
their memory. They take one look and stall.

The last shot shows four men crossing a bridge
in Machu Picchu and, in the reflection of the river,
a shadow bridge and four ancestral shadows crossing.

Dog Days

How beautiful she was
with her amber eyes
ears hemmed like silk purses
their insides soft as the petals of iris
her hound's high haunches
her poor docked stump of a tail.

How afraid she was
of the paper lampshade's ghostly shifting
of the dragon fire of hot-air balloons
of the vet's cold floor
of being alone.

How comforting she was
with her welcoming skid down the stairs
her grunts and snuffles in the creaky basket
her jump and flump on the bed
the collapse of legs, the warm dump
of herself, her dry biscuity smell,
her contented 'humph'.

How she could lift the heart
in exuberant take-off after a rabbit
how, for her, our going out
into field or wood, was a going home.
How elegant her trot, her point,
her pose on the seat in the window
how she was the book
of the children's childhood.

How long her dying took.

AUNT ROMA & CO

Aunt Roma

I thought her death romantic. TB, she only
nineteen and this loud silence growing about her.

By the time I was old enough to start asking
questions, the silence was inches thick. A nail
would glance off its walls. It was the size

of a temple. I wonder now how Roma wormed
her way into our lives. Was it her doing
that Grandma, crouching close to the fire

couldn't get warm? She who sent Grandad
urgently, nightly, off to the pub? Made
a hypochondriac of her brother, put weak lungs

into our medical records, made me dream
of sanatoriums set among pine trees
high in Swiss mountains? Where Roma

never went. Where you could hear
clear through the silence.

The Children's Tale

On his treacherous, miles-long journey
from the sewer to the plug-hole
of Mrs. Taylor, the class teacher's bath,
Sid the spider has a very hard time.
A rat nearly eats him. A gang
of cockroaches attack him. Narrowly
he escapes drowning under an avalanche
of water by hanging on a thread. Attempting
a wire trapeze he looses a leg. A passing
beetle mocks him. Bravely he labours on
in the dark and the wet and the stench.
The pipe to the plug-hole is steep
as the peak of Kilimanjaro. And just
as he crawls wearily up into the slippery,
icy whiteness of the bath, someone
turns on the shower. The visiting writer
has to rescue Sid, inventing a towel
flung over the side of the bath
so that Sid can clamber, seven-legged,
to safety, spin a nice warm web
in a nice warm corner of the linen cupboard.
Obligingly the children acquiesce
in the story that it is *they* who want
a happily-ever-after ending.

They start a new story about a snail
crunched, crushed and squelched
to slime by the lawn mower monster.

The Fishwoman

So grey I thought she'd risen from the sea
to trundle her cart over the cobbles
to Market Street. Never smiled. Wasn't
one of us. Could have been an ex-
mermaid in Neptune's thrall for breaking
sea rules or loving a mortal.

She was the first artist I ever knew.
How she could behead and gut a freckled-
bellied plaice, slit a kipper to a pair
of fine gloves. Pure origami her knack
of wrapping a haddock in a sheet of old news.
I never thought she dealt in death
only in mystery and accomplishment.

I venture that at night you'd see her
sail away, her cart a gull-drawn tub,
fish jumping to welcome her like children
and she a golden Aphrodite singing.

Potato Cuts

This is not potato country. Rice –
long grain, short, brown, white,
Basmati, *Uncle Ben's* – and pasta –
spaghetti, vermicelli, tagliatelli, but
potatoes, no. Only things passing as spuds,
sprouting and sweating in sticky plastic.

There are losses one learns to live with.
Horses and carts, a health service,
lovers, clean streets,
justice, an empire – possibly tobacco.
but potatoes, no. Which is why I've
grown this terrible nostalgia for *earlies*;

for that secret moment in the allotment
when we forked them up, archaeologically
jubilant; for those Sunday jaunts
with the kids to the potato fields;
for my mother mashing and boiling
entirely without reverence; for Sunday's
roasts; for Spring's butter and parsley;
for Grandad's chip butties. Oh for all
the tangled roots and attachments just
under the surface of unreachable childhood.

The Long Count

"The third calendar was the 'long count' which reckoned the number of days since the mythical beginning of the Mayan era."

Summer night at half mast
and the children away.
Their lost time-tables
have rolled up the difference
between night and day,
unpicked the stitches
of hours and minutes.

'The flesh is worn
as a daily thing, like the sun.'
I am wearing the sun
in British Summer Time
down the street
where old Mrs. Merry,
a glyph in her window,
does over-time.

Builders unplug rotten windows
and let out the wine. Something's
begun at the house two doors down
where a week ago (by the *haab* year)
a whole life was swilled down
by a Pickford's whale.

Now three unsettled cars shimmy
outside and a door stands open
on a pot of flowers. Presently
new people will come. Old
Mrs. Merry waves her hand,
a stitch in time.

To Kate at Twenty-Five

......at that terrible moment when the voice of the past is no longer
distant but quite as loud as the voice of the present.
                              Arthur Miller on *Death of a Salesman.*

I'm watching a bird that's flown
dangerously close to the house
flit in and out of the fuschia when
you 'phone, terror struck, to say
'twenty-five is undeniably grown-up'
which you always wanted to be
but now have doubts. Perhaps

because I'm fifty-four and anxious
to evade portentous dates
I drift in underwater time – head
in a book or out with the birds. Now
when I look up to where you are
it's like a change of climate.
Too hot. Too exposed. Not enough
foliage. It hurts to hear about it.
I want to say 'Regress! Come home!'
Send you Factor 15. My big umbrella.

But ever since your call it's as if
someone's swung a torch and shone its beam
in all the hidden corners of my life
or as if in one brief flash I'd seen
a single track – yours forward, mine back.

After

(i.m. my mother)

Two years after, and I think of you
still in the waiting room. If you'd arrived,
safely, you'd have let me know. Something
in the air would have told me so –
I'd have felt your contentment. But my guess
is limbo, where I see you waiting
in a bit of a huff at the lack of attention;
cracking a few jokes perhaps, about this
'not being much of a hotel. No room service,
and definitely not five star' – you
with the spotlights shinning about you.
'And all this blue,' you grumble,
'what's wrong with a nice rose pink?'

Well, what I think is that inside (only
it's not inside, more a kind of eternal
everywhere), the others – angels or whoever –
are wondering when you'll give up
being so down-to-earth. And I suspect
that the only closed door is your heart
which jammed shut – oh years and years ago
when he, your one love, died. And I bet
he's in there now, fretting and wishing
you'd hurry up. Remember how he used to say
of money, 'You can't take it with you
when you go'? Is it so, d'you think
with all we hang on to as the self?

And is it you or me that has to let go?

Waiting

On the dot of eleven-fifteen
I'd 'phone her. Sunday morning,
after *The Archers*, doing the dutiful
daughter bit. Knew she'd be waiting,
sat with a stack of mags and memories
under her cushion, watching the clock,
the blank telly, the long empty days.

I was glad of the distance. Hated
her waiting – for *him* to come home
to the dried-up dinner; for school
to finish; a night at the pictures;
two weeks in Sidmouth; husbands
for daughters; the doctor's visit;
time to pass, night to end.

Now she's upped sticks and eloped
with the loot of my childhood
and Sunday a.m. finds me fraught
as a homing pigeon thwarted of home.
All's latitude and longitude
And no north pole. No coo. All moan.
And the only voice I hear's my own

from years ago: running behind her
up the street, calling, 'Wait! Wait for me!'

My Father's Chandelier

It was love at first sight.
He bought the house that housed it.
At night it turned our hall
into the planetarium
or a Viennese ballroom poised
for Strauss waltzes. It was Europe
lighting up its candles,
my father's happy-ever-after
fairy tale. Mid-century my sister
danced her bridal night under it.

We sold it. It was too showy,
too difficult to clean. We had no room
for it and no heart. Now we go
for side lights, lights that cast shadows,
or those cheap, non-lasting paper shades
that shift and shake in the many draughts.

Yet still it shines in memory's dark,
my father's dream, a hanging basket of light,
impossible to put out.

International Trader

Died, only half-way through
the quest to *Waring & Gillow's* three piece suite
and the crystal chandelier and five-star holiday hotel
in Majorca and the captaincy of the golf club.
Died, saying 'there is still so much I want to do.'
Died, with your trilby still set north for treasure,
before I was ready,
before you were ready,
before I'd found another love,
while I was still trawling behind you,
you, the international trader
in that commodity persistence,
who told me to try and try
and try again.
And again.
And then didn't yourself
practice what you preached
but lay felled
by the first blow
flat on your back
with an oxygen mask clamped
on your mouth,
doing what you told me
never to do,

going out,
and slamming the door behind you.

Grandad

Holds court. It's his Saturday visit.
He's king-like in the carver,
his half-a-Guiness crowned with foam.
We're alone. Fat, purple worms
trapped under the skin of Grandad's hands
slither and wriggle. His eyes
are dissolving to water. The bumps
behind his ears could be the stubs
and start of horns. He holds
a shilling clenched in his paw, says
'We nearly drowned you when you were born.'
When he lets his false teeth fall
monstrously from his lips,
he's practising for the day
he turns into a gargoyle.

Grandma as a Genie

It happened in the middle of the school play.
I was a Chinese genie. 'Command
thy humble servant to appear', I said.
And did. It was then that Grandma vanished.

I'd given her the idea. I believe she jumped
into the urn she kept on the window sill
and which was so tall she could stand upright
inside it without in the least disturbing
the knife-sharp pleats of the skirt she wore.

Grandma liked things tidy. And provided
she kept her shoulders taut and her arms
in, she'd have fitted the urn very nicely.
I knew she was in there. Sharp-pleated
and furious. Nobody's humble servant.

Wives

I've just about placed him. Have the chronology
of his past pattable as a ball of pastry
you could roller-pin flat when 'My first wife...'
he says. Just like that. Lightly. As an aside.
A moment before the furniture in this house
looked perpetual. Now, from a continent ago,
in a gust of prairie wind, there's a young
Canadian bride at the door – her smile
is the children's framed on the mantel. Wife two's
impassive. Knows we all inhabit lives within
lives, countries another can never travel.

I think of you – at supper perhaps, in another
world – bundling up our sixteen years in that
light aside. And suddenly the letters of each word
lengthen as shadows do at dusk, and struck
like turning-forks against the heart, reverberate
and sink their shanks, their pothooks and hangers
home to dark. And there, tonight, though all the doors
of all my living rooms are shut, they moan, they moan.

Quite

You were my sweetest love and quite the hottest,
I liked your Cockney songs, your balding pate,
How sad it is that every passion rottest.

With lust and love I liked you quite a lottest,
Your nibbleable ears, your comfy weight,
You were my sweetest love and quite the hottest.

What joy you gave when lost in my dark forest,
I liked your stubby hands, your lazy gait,
How sad it is that every passion rottest.

I thought that you and I quite neatly fittest,
My dove-tailed love, my heart's fair duplicate,
You were my sweetest love and quite the hottest.

To ask if I was yours was not quite honest,
Your little lizard tongue made me your mate,
How sad it is that every passion rottest.

And now this bright bravado's all I've gottest,
I had in mind a more erotic fate,
You were my sweetest love and quite the hottest,
How sad it is that every passion rottest.

At Your Gate

The cabin's quite cosy. I don't
halloo much any more. Nor,
for fear she might answer, do I call
upon my soul. I pen the occasional
and rather formulaic canton but as for
singing in the dead of night
I gave that up when the neighbours complained.

I am happy, I assure you. I listen
to the babbling gossip of the internet,
the traffic on the reverberate by-pass.
I often think that my dream of bliss
would surely have been disappointed
whereas I have had years of pleasurable
anticipation, energising longing; purpose.

At least this is what I tell myself
when the willow creaks and the bed's cold.

Belonging

'You lack the sense of taking part.' Wislawa Szymborska

Sometimes your fingers find the spot
that springs the lock.
You can never do it twice.

Or a flower
suddenly looks back at you,

or opening the bonnet of the car
you lose your head to the engine,
forget what you are.

It's no good trying. The knack
is to be taken by surprise,
swept off your feet
not in some distant place
but where you are.

Love does it, of course
though more rarely than we'd wish

and death's sure fire.

INNOCENCE & EXPERIENCE

Milk

Fifty years I've been downing the stuff
and now can't take it. It's like
the final loss of innocence, the end
of that imagined England where out there,
somewhere, were moo-cows who loved me,
and Tess, in her dairy, rested
one flushed young cheek against a warm flank,
and children in winter playgrounds
daily drank virtue from dinky bottles
and all heartache was softened
by a mugful warmed and sweetened with sugar.

How shall I live without the song of the milk float,
morning's clink of new hope
and Frank on the doorstep calling me 'darling'?

Drinking Brandy on Whitstable Beach

(for Naomi and Tim)

As if this is what I was meant for
and it's taken forever to find place
and vocation. I'm swashbuckling, hearty
and fresh from the sea. Over
the sea-honed stones, exultant I crunch
in my old-salt's boots. It's sure
stones, sea's sting and brandy's burn
that I love, sitting and swigging
on a groyne that won't last; facing
the music with a big globed glass
in my gladly cold hand. Happy at last,
drinking brandy on Whitstable beach.

All those childhood years spent
watching the men gargle the strong
stuff and now I've the art
of the fragile goblet, the magic draught:
two fingers either side the stem;
globe in palm; the lingering,
appreciative swirl and sniff before
the first sip, then the fire
in the throat, fierce as a kiss.
O I could make a career out of this,
drinking brandy on Whitstable beach.

HOMES & GARDENS

Estimates

(for Tim Ward)

The first makes inscrutable notes in a small red book,
probes soft wood with his key, says he's not
doing much at the moment and no, he doesn't work
to Radio One, he likes to listen to what's
going on in his head. That's why he does this job.
He pauses at a painting in the hall,
remarks the canvas needs re-stretching.
He shakes my hand and calls me 'Mrs'.

The second's a double act. *Inca Developments* bring me
a brochure of photos and letters from satisfied
clients – 'Last year I has my loft converted...
the mess and disturbance was next to nothing.' The Incas
are trendy. The handsome one laughs at a book on my
desk.
They measure and map on a serious clip-board,
shake professional heads, voice expensive warnings.

The third's so tall he won't need a ladder. He finds
my house by guess-work having forgotten
the number. 'It's fifty-two', I say 'like weeks
in the year'. He says he thought there were fifty-six.
He takes neither notes nor measurements, looks
at the white-washed wall of the cellar, now grimed
with coal dust, and sees a landscape of mountains.

I try to estimate who I could bear to have
in the house for three whole weeks; worry about
what programmes the first man hears in his head;

check up on Inca myths (in which caves and sacrifice
feature quite largely) and think, perhaps,
I'd be most at home with the one who sees
mountain landscapes in cellars of coal dust
and doesn't yet know the length of the years.

The Painters

They appear like acrobats or clowns,
a troupe of them, all in white.
They've come to transform us.

Singing and whistling they travel lightly
up and down ladders in heavy boots.
Their brushes lap tenderly

at our walls, paint over the past.
Each morning there's a skim of oil
and water filming the paint.

They stir it in, bring colour back
like health. At lunch they bask
in the greenhouse on sunbeds

of paint sheets among pots of tomatoes,
share mugs of tea on our Costa del Sol.
When they leave we hardly dare

live in the new world they've left us. Lack
a matching virtue. Miss the theatricals,
the beach bums gracing our greenhouse,
the colour they brought to our lives.

Angus

Arrives with a hump
of sorrow on his back
that he defies anyone
to lift. It's his.
He's hanging on to it.

Tea, chat, sympathy,
nothing will coax a smile.
Within days the rot
in the attic is just our ruse
to ruin his life. He wants
to build kitchens, cathedrals,
a new ark. Possibly coffins.

Does an immaculate job.
Leaves us (unsmiling) with new
cleanly crafted floorboards.
But what shall we do
with the gloom that seeps from
wood, walls, beams?

Lowry's House

'It's too big you know – I mean life, sir' L. S. Lowry

Bleak. That's what everyone called it,
the stone house in Mottram-in-Longdendale,
the very name of the place having the chill
of rigor mortis. Inside, small dark rooms,
fourteen clocks all telling a different time,
portraits of the parents, Rossetti's girls,
a studio at the back, no carpet on the stairs,
no number on the 'phone. 'Cold as a monk's cell'
the rooms upstairs and the hall where at the end
he fell. Outside, a garden never entered,
waist high with weeds and grass.

Could we, to comfort ourselves, pretend,
his true home was the Manchester streets,
Salford College of Art, the Easter Fair
at Daisy Nook and not this stone retreat,
the company of clocks, awful thoughts,
the missing of mother, oils? No, *this*
was home, the drab bleak house of art,
where he never meant to stay, then found
he couldn't leave; where no-one
really lives, though the canvases persist
in telling us how vibrantly we did.

Bulbs

Like an addict in need of supplies, I buy bags
and bags of them. They nuzzle each other
inside the brown paper. I've a lust for them
like a pregnant woman for a certain food.

I set them out on the kitchen table. The raw
light hurts them. They want to be snugged
in the moist, dark bed. The root
of this daffodil is like several dead spiders.

This crocus is postmarked with a small brown
sun. They wear thread-bare vests of pencil-
shavings, darned with dark soil from their past
earth lives. Some have a small white fang

at the tip. I don't want to plant them. I'd
like to leave them, as candles keeping vigil
in the night; hold one in my heart all winter.

Apple Sense

To live with an apple tree
in your garden is not
to understand it. Today,
for example, it stands
on one leg, answers
February's ice with a snarl
of black spikes. In summer
its leaves are tarnished,
its fruit beyond reach.
There's an exchange going on
between light, weather,
time and tree in which I'm
a by-stander, asker
of inane questions
in the wrong language.

The tree's rhythm, for
example – bough's rise
and fall – was it learnt
from the sea? Does it mind
that what was orchard
is now city street? Has it
Eden in its genes? Who
is it here for? Balance
and symmetry – imposed or
chosen – seem what it's about,
though the more I look
the less I know. It's
as though some extra sense,
an apple sense, were needed,
a cure for sight's blindness,
an ear for sap, a way
of speaking in blossom.

Eve Makis the Abject Serpent Serviable

(with apologies to William Dunbar)

Thogh wel I wis Adam it was
Quho in Eden durit gret distres
(Also muche doolie baill and sore heid-ake)
For to gif eche fishe and foull a name –
Yit leift was it to me to tame
The sle and sely serpent crewall
Aresten him of mortall stang
And haf him eatyn fro my hande.

In wyntir in a gardin strang
Sneir I his rumpillis on yron frame.
Yit I in symmer let him glyid
Gruncheing on his fronsit wame
Al slyk and slyding in the grassis –
Veramant I wis al his gamountis
And mak of thame my swete ballatis.

Thogh boundin alway to my tappe,
Bisily his heid I wagge
Til he with mony balmy schouris
Drenchis al my lusty flouris.

abject = outcast
baill = sorrow
duren = endured
doolie = sad, doleful
fronsit = wrinkled
gamountis = capers
gruncheing = grumbling
sneir = spin
rumpillis = rough folds
verament = indeed, certainly
wame = belly

Monterey Pine

You can't choose the trees you live with.
You open your eyes and find them,
there, like parents. This Monterey Pine
I've lived with now for nine
whole years, I'd never have chosen.

How did it get here, this huge
American cowboy, crowned
with an over-large stetson, all bouncy-
boughed and throwing its weight around?
Its proper place is high
and dry in the coastal slopes
of California, guarding the ocean.
Here, in my scrap of city garden,
It's grown delusions, thinks
it's a penthouse for pigeons,
a tenement for rooks.

It's an albatross.

Great big lumbering thing,
taking all the light.
Tossing and turning at night.
Requiring a tree surgeon every
five years. Leaning at an angle
that alarms the Insurance.
Needing to be rescued
from ivy's clutches. Knowing
the weather through the tips
of its needles. Confidante
of darkness, rain and wind.
Keeper of their secrets. No,

I'd not have chosen this tree
that has so bountifully given
its rhythms, its rightful notions
of time, its green, its hush;
its ocean dream; its love.

When my mind's a stone in which
memories, like fossils, hide,
if you could break it open,
among the things you'd find,
is a drop of the Pacific
and a shoot of Monterey Pine.

Weeding Mrs. Baker's Garden

She has four hardy daughters,
four stout sons-in-law (to match)
and a biannual crop
of grand-children.
they should weed her garden.

The man next door
is an acupuncturist and healer
(of sorts). He should lay hands
on it. Two doors down, a flamboyant
girl with a tangle of curls
rides a yellow land-rover
all over the county
preaching to farmers
about acid rain
and caring for Nature
but not Mrs. Baker

whose pre-Raphaelite tangle
of weeds is the work
of the artist Neglect
or Mrs. Baker herself
who, after all, has not always
been eighty-five.

She should not
have given away the spade
to one of the four hardies
or said, as she must have done
when her Roland died,
'That was his job, not mine',
so that instead of growing
she went on narrowing

and the garden died
where Roland had grown roses
and clematis and edged
the little paths with bricks
neatly marked in blanket stitch
that now you can't find.

No-one can expect *me*
to weed Mrs. Baker's garden.
I have not been here
long enough to grow obligations.
Roland shall not speak to me
through the ouiji board
about forget-me-nots,
pansies, death and its sly
creeping take-over.

* * * *

I took my spade and hoe
and I raked Death over
in Mrs. Baker's garden,
and Mrs. Baker said
my breasts would grow
with all that digging.
Probably I shall go
sooner
than Mrs. Baker.

Now the four hardy daughters
all hate me
for what they think is kindness.
But I lie flat on my back
in bed with possibly a slipped disc
playing a rag on a foxglove saxophone
to the cheated skies.

A FEW STRANGE CREATURES

The Cullen Skink

If the temperature's right
you might see him out
in a very fine suit
of the best bravado,
but skinking with caution
for his eyesight's poor
and he's all out of proportion.

Unshelled, in the buff,
his raw-pink skin
is prone to shrinkage
which is why he lets no-one in
and lives far north, alone
in a nest of coddled mementoes
kept on simmer. Some say
it's the Cullen Skink's nature
to shiver and to be perpetually
on the brink of some great thought
he never delivers.

He likes to drink.
He likes to look at the moon.
At night you can hear the clink
as he walks the jetty
trailing a kind of umbilical cord,
the dried-up remnants
of wings, fur, paws.

* Cullen Skink – a Scottish recipe for smoked haddock

At Last I Decide to Speak to Fear Directly...

Fear, I said, I want you out of my house,
I'm sick of your chilling, clinging habits,
the way you fatten yourself on darkness.

Fear sniggered. He was squatting, squint-
eyed in a corner, totting up tomorrow's dangers.
How can you turn me out? he asked.
I'm yours. Remember our early days?
'Mind how you cross the road. Don't
speak to strangers?' You were all ears.
I was useful then. For a moment
Fear looked quite pathetic.

You're not now, I said. You've grown
too big for your shadow. You're eating me
out of heart and hope. I wake in the morning
to find you've underlined all the worst bits
in the paper. You've thought up ten new diseases.

I work all night, admitted Fear.
That's another thing, I said. I've noticed
how you shrivel in sunshine.
I'm thin-skinned, whined Fear. *Sunshine hurts.*
And when friends come you hide in the loft.
Embarrassed, said Fear.
You've tricked me this way before, I said,
with your poor-little-me act. I know you.
Soon you'll be stuffing your mouth with obituaries
and torture trials. You should write horror scripts.
Fear grinned. *Too busy.* he said.

Not any more, I said. As of now you're
unemployed. I'm pensioning you off.
Fear looked hurt. *Your forgetting,* he said,

all the times I've protected you, saved you ...
from lives I might have led, adventures
I might have ventured ...
Death by drowning, earthquake, heart-break, chanted Fear.
There you go again, I said. I must advise you
I've invited Risk to stay.

*Mind how you cross the road. Don't
speak to strangers,* whispered Fear
sliding back under the bed.

The Enemy

The one
who jumps out of the dark
of memory, lurks in a doorway
has your number.

Whose boots thud over your soul,
whose fist hammers your heart.

Whose integrity, love and trust
you never doubted.

Who feeds you despair
crushed in a teaspoon.

Who slits your throat, leaves you to die,
combs his hair, adjusts his tie.

Who has nothing against you *personally*.

Who hates children.

Who arrives after the war,
after the heart by-pass and the car crash
to kick you downstairs.

The one you find
when you've bolted all doors

waiting inside.

Viva Health Club Blues

At a certain time of day
they play Elgar's Cello Concerto.
I'm in the gym, doing ten minutes
(at 4 mph) on the treadmill, thinking
of Jacqueline du Pré. Sometimes I swim
to Chopin – his *Fantaisie-Impromptu
in C sharp minor, Opus 66.*
Twenty lengths and his heartache's
no better. Aloft on the exercise bikes
there's plug-in earphones and a choice
of four channels. (Everyone wears
that listening-in look babies wear
when shitting their nappies.) In the bar
there are paper palm trees and vegan salads
The slogan on the sports team's T-shirts
reads: 'We take your fitness personally'.

O Viva! Viva! Viva those guardians
of my cardiovascular condition
Elgar, Jacqueline, Chopin – and tonight
Ella, soothing my stretch marks
With *I've got you under my skin.*

MYSTERIES

Reconstructing Heaven

I'd like to keep it in my imaginary empire
of dreamy places – the Garden of Eden,
the Promised Land, the Elysian Fields –
not let it go like a country that's won
independence, refound its culture, sent
me home. Reconstructing the self's easy compared
to changing the picture I fixed about seven
where the landscape's medieval and vaguely
Italian and there's buttercupped meadows
and they speak only Latin. People in black
(despite the weather) lounge by the river
looking faintly ecstatic. I don't know how
to find anyone, or if I want to.

I could, perhaps, rustle up an ocean,
add dogs and a camera obscura focused
on earth. But somehow the place is stuck
in memory's immutable mud. I feel as I did
on holiday in Bournemouth as a kid.
Miserably awkward. Not knowing how
to be happy. How to fit in.

Guide Book Angels (Wells Cathedral)

I feel for them,
the Nine Orders of Angels
described in the guide book
as 'badly weathered'.

Cherub, Seraph, Throne.

Not long ago they were dancing
in Dante's Paradiso,
nine fiery circles ringing
a single radiant point.

Power, Virtue, Domination.

'Barely recognisable', it's said,
the crowd the shepherds saw,
the one Mary met,
those sometimes UFO's to us.

Principality, Archangel, Angel.

I feel for them,
the Nine Orders of Angels,
time-worn, exhausted by travel
and hosannas; the weighing of souls,
the to-ing and fro-ing with prayers,
yet holding behind them, folded in shadow,
(like waiting love, or what matters most),
the fling of their lovely disorderly wings,
still 'in good condition', still lavishly crimson.

Without You

I miss the pictures of you in the house –
the stable steamy with sweet straw
and donkey's breath; the baby photos
in you mother's lap and then the handsome
curly-headed lad with bleeding heart
and lantern held aloft. The fisherman
of men; wonder-worker; stuntman
walking on the water; table-turner;
raiser of the dead. You, resigned,
in wine-red robe at the nightmare
supper table. Then carrying the load.
The scapegoat of the cross. The mocking
crown of thorns. The hanging head.

All gone. All lost. All sold.
At best, a metaphor. At worst a story.
And you like one of the family
sent abroad. The house is not the same
without you. Not quite home.

Arkadi Monastery

1.
All week your heart's been battered
by the three infinities – mountain
sea and sky – so now you take the bus
out of the roistering town and climb
hill upon hill, through healing olive
groves and up such narrow windings
you wish for a bus of bendable rubber.
A halt, close on some scraggy edge
of eternity has you closing your eyes
while the driver plays bouzouki music
nice and loud and adds hoots (animato)
and smiles in his mirror from which
hangs his insurance – the Virgin Mary,
(in a ring of glass diamonds); a Phaistos
disc; a bright blue eye, primitive and plastic.

2.
And when you arrive at what feels like the top –
only there are more hills, further and beyond –
and the bus goes asthmatically off, you find
yourself high on a hill with its top
like a hard-boiled egg sliced off and it's dusty
and silent and sunny and your heart lifts off
like a plane from the runway. The quietness is such
it's as though your ears were suddenly cleared
of the world. You hear bees in the gorse; see,
among musical goats, a grave-bearded one pacing
precisely along a wall as if telling his beads.
So what you're aware of first of all
is the dusk peach walls, the orange trees,
the light and shade of cloistered walks,
the vines at their windings, a homely log stack,
a mop at a door, the one-armed nun (the tourists'
favourite), a glimpse of a monk tending carnations,

and within the courtyard, the peach's dark kernel,
the church where beeswax candles drip their prayers.
Like Jacob's ladder the bell-rope's graceful drop to earth.

3.
In the musuem the past lies peaceful under glass.
You view the monks' embroidered vestments;
'the toilsome work of Parthenios Koitzas'; read,
in painstaking chronicles, random extracts
about the shortage of bread (up two piastres),
the arrival, in Chania, of four hundred two-masters
from Constantinople; the spread of the plague;
the earthquake they thought was the end of the world.
At his desk the museum attendant sells souvenirs
while with one hand he trails black, lascivious
worry beads over his girl assistant's naked thighs.

4.
The guide book takes you on a different tour –
points out the bullet holes in the refectory door,
the tables and benches gashed by sword;
leads to the gunpowder store and the November night
when the Cretan freedom fighters –
choosing death before surrender to the Turks –
fired at the kegs and blew themselves sky-high.
Distant as myth, these heroes and martyrs
'Who in their transcendent struggle conquered death'.
Even as the terms alarm your post-war nerves
the heart, instinctive, leaps to rampaging desire
for love, belief – an enemy to test you at the limits
of the self. Tourists keep cameras bandaged
to their eyes and you, in self-defence, turn history
to a film show in the head. Scan cannon fire,
rearing horse, pall of smoke, outnumbered Greeks,
Turks breaking down the door. Then the courtyard
carnage and the sound-track's awful noise.
The cast is good. Goat-bearded Abbot Gabriel

whose head they skewered ear to ear and the handsome
Konstantine Giaboudakis whose pistol fired the kegs.

'God's fire' they called the flames that dark
November night Arkadi burned. Is this what passion is?
This two-way charge? The spit on which our hearts
are turned? On shelves more suitable for china
there's a line-up of the heroes' sword-hacked skulls
and a woman's freshly braided, morning coil of hair.

5.
You fill your water bottle from the courtyard's tap.
Drink grace. Lie under the trees. Hear the pine cones
popping in the heat and take the bus back down.
The woman who plumps herself beside you on the seat
settles a bag abloom with white carnations on her lap.
She gives you one. All night it scents your room.

Jubilee Line

It looks highly dangerous.
They should put up a notice –
**KISSING ON THE ESCALATOR
STRICTLY FORBIDDEN.**

See these two? She's perched
on the step above him
leaning down to his mouth,
close to falling, wobbling,
laughing. And he –
he hardly knows which step
to stand on. She's bending down
and the escalator's going up –
is she actually standing on one leg? –
and I think they're trying
to be what's called 'as one'.

They could topple at any moment
and we'd all go down like ninepins.
The whole risky adventure's against
the laws of gravity. You'd think
they'd consider the rest of us
for whom holding on, keeping
to the side, now seems ridiculous.